HUMPBACK
WHALES

Printed in Hong Kong

96   97   98   99   00   5   4   3   2   1

Library of Congress Cataloging-in-Publication Data

Clapham, Phil.
    Humpback whales / Phil Clapham.
        p.   cm. – (WorldLife library)
    Includes bibliographical references (p.72)
    ISBN 0-89658-296-5
    1. Humpback whale.   I. Title.   II. Series.
QL737.C424C58   1996
599.5'1–dc20   95–46052
                                                            CIP

Distributed in Canada by Raincoast Books, 8680 Cambie Street, Vancouver, B.C. V6P 6M9

Published by Voyageur Press, Inc.
123 North Second Street, P.O. Box 338, Stillwater, MN 55082 U.S.A.
612-430-2210, fax 612-430-2211

Please write or call, or stop by, for our free catalog of natural history publications. Our toll-free
number to place an order or to obtain a free catalog is 800-888-WOLF (800-888-9653).

Educators, fundraisers, premium and gift buyers, publicists, and marketing managers:
Looking for creative products and new sales ideas? Voyageur Press books are available at special
discounts when purchased in quantities, and special editions can be created to your
specifications. For details contact the marketing department.

Photographs © 1996:

Front Cover© Michio Hoshino (Minden Pictures)
Back Cover © Colin Baxter
Page 1   © Andy Rouse (NHPA)
Page 4   © Michio Hoshino (Minden Pictures)
Page 6   © David B Fleetham (Oxford Scientific Films)
Page 8   © Michio Hoshino (Minden Pictures)
Page 9   © David B Fleetham (Oxford Scientific Films)
Page 10   © Flip Nicklin (Minden Pictures)
Page 13   © Bryan & Cherry Alexander (NHPA)
Page 14   © Colin Baxter
Page 15   © Mark Carwardine (Bruce Coleman Ltd)
Page 17   © Flip Nicklin (Minden Pictures)
Page 18   © Jeff Foott Productions (Bruce Coleman Ltd)
Page 19   © Michio Hoshino (Minden Pictures)
Page 20   © Clive Bromhall (Oxford Scientific Films)
Page 22   © Mark Carwardine (Bruce Coleman Ltd)
Page 23   © Andy Rouse (NHPA)
Page 25   © Tony Martin (Oxford Scientific Films)

Page 26   © Jeff Foott Productions (Bruce Coleman Ltd)
Page 28   © Michio Hoshino (Minden Pictures)
Page 29   © Flip Nicklin (Minden Pictures)
Page 31   © Ben Osborne (Oxford Scientific Films)
Page 32   © Daniel J Cox (Oxford Scientific Films)
Page 34   © Center for Coastal Studies
Page 36   © Michio Hoshino (Minden Pictures)
Page 38   © Michio Hoshino (Minden Pictures)
Page 39   © Jeff Foott Productions (Bruce Coleman Ltd)
Page 41   © Roger Tidman (NHPA)
Page 42   © Michio Hoshino (Minden Pictures)
Page 43   © Duncan Murrell (Oxford Scientific Films)
Page 44   © Howard Hall (Oxford Scientific Films)
Page 47   © Clive Bromhall (Oxford Scientific Films)
Page 48   © Doug Perrine (Planet Earth Pictures)
Page 50   © Flip Nicklin (Minden Pictures)
Page 53   © Flip Nicklin (Minden Pictures)
Page 54   © Flip Nicklin (Minden Pictures)

Page 57   Top Left © Center for Coastal Studies
              Top Right © Center for Coastal Studies
              Bottom Left © Center for Coastal Studies
              Bottom Right © Center for Coastal Studies
Page 58   © Tony Martin (Oxford Scientific Films)
Page 59   © Jeff Jacobsen
Page 60   © Richard Kolar (Oxford Scientific Films)
Page 61   © Tsuneo Nakamura (NHPA)
Page 62   © Duncan Murrell (Oxford Scientific Films)
Page 64   © Tony Martin (Oxford Scientific Films)
Page 65   © Neil Bromhall (Oxford Scientific Films)
Page 66   © Bryan & Cherry Alexander (NHPA)
Page 67   © Ken Balcomb (Bruce Coleman Ltd)
Page 68   © Center for Coastal Studies
Page 69   © Phil Clapham
Page 71   © Flip Nicklin (Minden Pictures)

HUMPBACK
WHALES

Phil Clapham

Voyageur Press

Contents

Humpback Whales

He is the most gamesome and light-hearted of all the whales, making more
gay foam and white water than any other of them
(Herman Melville: Moby Dick)

On a windless morning in February, the sun rises over calm waters off the coast of a Caribbean island. A small sailing craft gently rocks at anchor as the couple on board wake from their night's sleep. As they open their eyes, they hear strange noises coming through the boat's hull. Long moans and sweeps of sound echo through the surrounding water. Curious, they climb to the deck. They see nothing to explain the haunting sounds that can still be heard coming faintly through the surface. On an impulse, the woman dives into the water. Immediately she feels the full force of the sound, now so loud that her rib cage vibrates from the power of the lower notes. Afraid but strangely exhilarated, she returns to the surface and talks of her extraordinary experience in such excited terms that the man dives in to share it. Moments later, as they return to the boat, a loud whoosh! nearby startles them. Turning, they see the sleek black back of a humpback whale at the surface 50 m away. He breathes five times, his blow hanging like mist in the cool morning air. Then, as the whale arches his back and dives, the great tail rises gracefully into the air and slips beneath the surface.

Scenes such as this have marked humankind's contact with humpback whales for centuries. From the earliest times, coastal peoples have marvelled at the animals' immense size and power as they leaped from the water in spectacular breaching displays. Or, as in the case of the couple on the yacht, mariners have heard the haunting song that males sing to attract females.

Sometimes these experiences inspired fear or awe: the humpback must certainly have played a role in establishing a mythology that spoke darkly of sea monsters, and of sirens singing strange songs that lured sailors to their deaths. But all too often, especially in later years, the whales inspired another emotion: greed. By the 18th century the humpback whale was seen primarily as a source of profit, whose oil could be used to light lamps, and whose baleen could be turned into an array of products from combs to corset stays. More recently, fully mechanized commercial whaling reduced the worldwide population of humpback whales by as much as 95%. A species that has filled the world's oceans with its beautiful song for perhaps seven million years was almost wiped out in fewer than a hundred.

With the cessation of commercial whaling and the growth of the environmental movement, humpback whales have begun to recover, and we have once again begun to appreciate the living, rather than the dead, animal. We are awed by the humpback's size and behavior, touched by its occasional curiosity about us, and enchanted by its songs. More and more people have come into contact with humpback whales through a growing whalewatching industry, and a new mythology has emerged. We see humpbacks as highly intelligent (which they probably are not). We think of them as gentle giants (which they certainly are towards us, but often not towards each other). But they have also

Some diving humpbacks arch their backs to reveal the humped appearance from which their name derives.

become a symbol of our fight to save the Earth; and rightly so, since if we cannot save some of the largest and most magnificent creatures ever to live on the planet, then it reflects what a poor state the world is in.

In recent years, much research has been conducted on living humpback whales. Long-term studies of identified individuals have taught us much about this fascinating species. This book draws on current knowledge to paint an introductory portrait of the humpback whale, and tries to show that humpbacks do not need the baggage of romantic human ideas with which we sometimes try to burden them. They are sufficiently remarkable in their own right.

Cetaceans

The humpback whale is one of the 78 species of whales, dolphins and porpoises that exist in the modern world. Together, they are known as cetaceans (pronounced "se-TAY-shuns"). The term comes from *ketos*, an ancient Greek word for whale that is still in use today. Like us, cetaceans are mammals: they breathe air, give birth to live young, and nurse those young with milk. They comprise a great variety of animals that inhabit all of the world's oceans, and several of its largest rivers. The range of sizes found within the group is large. At one end of the scale is the tiny vaquita, a species of porpoise that is no more than 1.5 m (five feet) in length. At the other end is the giant blue whale which, at up to 33.5 m (110 feet) and 190 tons, is the largest animal ever to have lived in the history of our planet.

Of all the marine mammals, cetaceans are the most completely adapted to life in an aquatic environment. They represent the end result of a long process of evolution which began more than 60 million years ago. The ancestor of all cetaceans was a small and rather undistinguished-looking mammal called a condylarth. The condylarth was also the ancestor of the ungulates, the group that includes hooved mammals such as deer, sheep and cows. Today, the ungulates are the cetaceans' closest living relatives on land, a fact which has recently been confirmed by DNA studies.

Quite how a small four-legged land animal evolved into the wide range of sleek aquatic creatures that we find in the oceans today is not entirely clear, but we can trace the general process with reasonable certainty. Fossils tell us that the transition was gradual, and in the early stages it involved animals which inhabited river estuaries or the margins of warm, shallow seas. For these early mammals, the aquatic realm must have represented an abundant source of food, and perhaps a refuge from predators on land.

As the early ancestors of whales spent more and more time in the sea, they developed specialized adaptations which made their aquatic existence easier. Over millions of years, many changes occurred. The body took on a sleek, hydrodynamic shape. The hind legs disappeared, while the forelimbs became modified into paddle-like flippers. A horizontal tail, powered by large muscles, developed for efficient propulsion. The bones became light and porous, since in water they no longer had to support the animal's weight as they would on land. With all these changes came a series of complex adaptations designed to provide the animal with the ability to dive, sometimes for long periods or to great depth. These included an increased capacity for oxygen (particularly in the muscles), placement of the nostrils on the top of the head to make breathing at the surface easier, and a remarkable network of valves which allowed the animal to deal with the problems of great pressure that arise with increasing depth.

The final transition to completely aquatic animals occurred approximately 45-50 million years ago. These first cetaceans, called archaeocetes, included a wide range of forms, both large and small. All are long since extinct, but they gave rise to the lineages that led to modern cetaceans.

Although whales today possess all of the adaptations mentioned above, they show considerable variation in the design and efficiency of these features. For example, some whales are much sleeker than others. The huge fin whale (second in size only to the blue) is as streamlined as a torpedo, with the speed to match: fin whales can reach burst speeds of 46 km an hour (25 knots, or nautical miles per hour). By contrast, the ponderous right whale is rotund and slow. Similarly, the range of cetacean diving abilities is wide: most porpoises can dive for only a few minutes at most, while the great sperm whale can remain submerged for over two hours. In addition, sperm whales dive to extraordinary depths: recent research has shown that they can travel to utterly lightless regions of the ocean more than 2000 m (7000 feet) below the surface.

Modern cetaceans carry with them vestiges of their terrestrial ancestry. Examine the internal structure of a whale's flipper and you will find that it looks like a huge hand, complete with finger bones. All whales possess the internal remnants of a (functionless) pelvis, and hind leg bones, and there are even rare cases of whales being

The humpback's dorsal fin is small. One of its principal functions is as a
heat exchanger: blood flow to the fin is increased when the whale is too warm. Researchers can
recognise an individual by the size and shape of its dorsal fin. Many humpback whales have very
scarred or battered fins, which make identification particularly easy.

Although smaller than the giant blue and fin whales, humpbacks are still among the largest animals ever to have lived on Earth, reaching a maximum length of about 18 m and weights of perhaps 50 tons.

born with vestigial hind limbs, an evolutionary throwback.

The cetaceans that we find in the world's oceans today are divided into two groups, or sub-orders. These are the odontocetes, or toothed whales, and the mysticetes, or baleen whales. As the name implies, the odontocetes (from dont, "tooth" and cetus/ketos, "whale") comprise all the cetaceans with teeth, including dolphins and porpoises as well as a rather mysterious group of deep-diving animals named the beaked whales. The sperm whale is the largest of all the toothed whales at 21 m (70 feet). The odontocetes also include the river dolphins, a fascinating group of animals that live in large watercourses such as the Amazon, the Ganges and the Yangtse, as well as in some large lakes. A remarkable feature of toothed whales is their development of a highly advanced biological sonar system for short-range navigation and finding food.

The humpback's powerful tail drives the animal on its long migrations. In the largest whales, the tails can be 5 m wide.

In contrast to the odontocetes, baleen whales like the humpback have no teeth. Instead, the mouth contains hundreds of plates of baleen, or whalebone. Despite the name, "whalebone" is not bone at all, but keratin, the same protein that makes up our hair and fingernails. The hard, triangular baleen plates are arranged in two long racks that hang from each side of the whale's upper jaw, and together they create an elaborate filtration system. When a humpback whale is feeding, it first takes a huge volume of water and food into its mouth, then uses its tongue to expel the water through the baleen. Unlike the water, the food cannot pass through the fine mesh of hair that fringes the inner surface of the baleen. Once all the water has been flushed out, the whale simply swallows its prey.

Baleen seems to have appeared at least 40 million years ago, in cetaceans whose ancestors had teeth. Its development allowed the whales to exploit the most abundant food in the ocean: small schooling fish and even smaller animal plankton. (*Plankton* is the name given to the innumerable species of tiny plants and animals that drift with the tides and currents.) Rather than chasing relatively large individual prey items (as sperm whales do with squid, or dolphins with fish), baleen whales can engulf entire schools of small creatures, which they literally sieve from the water. In fact, they are incapable of swallowing prey of any significant size: while a baleen whale's mouth is truly cavernous, its throat is very narrow, and even the largest blue whales have a gullet that is no more than a few inches wide.

While all mysticetes (the word means "moustached whale") have baleen, the size and form of this critical feature vary between species. Some of the baleen plates of minke whales are only 7 or 8 cm (a few inches) in length, while those of the bowhead (an arctic species related to the right whale) can reach an incredible 4.2 m (14 feet). The largest baleen plates in humpback whales are about 1.5 m (5 feet) long.

Although there is much debate in biology about how to define a species, eleven species of baleen whales are currently recognized. These are grouped into three families, the right whales, the grey whale (alone in a separate family), and a family of six species known as balaenopterids, or "rorquals". The humpback belongs to this last group. All rorquals have a series of pleats on the underside, stretching from the tip of the lower jaw to the navel (the word rorqual comes from the Danish *rør hval*, meaning "tubed whale"). When the whale is feeding, these pleats expand like an accordion, allowing the animal to greatly increase the capacity of its mouth.

Five species of rorqual are similar enough in body form and other features to be placed together in one subgroup, or genus, called *Balaenoptera*. This includes the blue, fin, minke, sei and Bryde's whale. The humpback, while sharing many features with these species, is sufficiently different to be assigned to its own subgroup within the rorqual family: the genus *Megaptera*.

A humpback's blow rises high into the air.
With each breath, a humpback will exchange about 90% of the
contents of its lungs, a respiratory rate that is five to six times
more efficient than that of humans.

Winged Whale

Several physical features set humpback whales apart from other rorquals. They are rather less sleek in form, and as a result are the slowest members of the family. On a few occasions, I have seen humpbacks accelerate to about 22-24 km an hour (12 or 13 knots) for short bursts, but this is rare, and they generally adopt a much more leisurely pace. Humpbacks are also unique in having many bumps, called tubercles, on their heads. The tubercles are connected to a rich network of nerves, and each tubercle contains a single stiff hair called a vibrissa, which is rather like a cat's whisker. The tubercles almost certainly have a sensory function, but quite what is unclear.

The most obvious difference, however, between humpbacks and other rorquals is their flippers. At almost a third of the length of the whale's body, these are proportionately the longest pectoral fins of any cetacean. In large adults, they can reach lengths of 5.2 m (17 feet). These huge appendages, like giant wings, have given the humpback its scientific name, *Megaptera novaeangliae*: the "big wing of New England". The latter part of the name acknowledges the fact that the first specimen to be formally described, in 1781, came from the northeastern United States.

The humpback is a moderately large baleen whale, small in comparison to its giant cousins the blue and fin, but still easily one of the largest animals on earth. The largest recorded humpback whale measured 19 m (62 feet). At this length, the whale would have weighed approximately 45 to 50 tons. As with all mysticetes, females are the larger of the two sexes. The difference, while not large, is consistent: adult female humpbacks are typically up to about a meter (three feet) longer than males. Why females should be larger is unclear, but it may relate to a general principle in mammalian reproduction that "bigger mothers are better mothers". The high energy cost of nursing in this species, together with the need to spend long periods in cold water, may have favored large size for both milk production and heat conservation. Other than size, there are few obvious

Various theories have attempted to explain why humpback whales evolved such large flippers: they range from greater manoeuverability to assistance with heat loss in warm water.

differences between the sexes though females have a lobe the size of grapefruit in their genital area; this lobe is absent in males, so if the underside of a humpback can be clearly seen it is possible to determine its sex.

Like all cetaceans, humpbacks possess a thick layer of fat, or blubber, beneath their skin. The blubber insulates the animal, allowing it to live in comfort even in frigid polar waters, in which most land mammals would die rapidly from hypothermia. Blubber is also a portable larder: humpbacks build up their fat stores during the summer feeding season, and must subsist entirely upon this reserve during the winter months, when they do not feed. The blubber layer in the largest humpbacks is about 15 cm (6 inches) thick. By some standards, this is not particularly large: bowhead whales, which spend most of their lives in the Arctic, can have as much as 60 cm (24 inches) of blubber.

All baleen whales have two nostrils, or blowholes, which are opened and closed with powerful muscles. A raised splashguard ahead of the blowholes keeps water out.

One other feature of the humpback whale deserves mention, since it has been the basis of much research on this species. When a humpback dives deeply, it frequently arches its back and raises its huge tail high in the air; this behavior is often called fluking, since another name for a whale's tail is its fluke. On the underside of a humpback's tail is a pattern of black and white markings that is unique to that individual. Just like a fingerprint, no two fluke patterns are exactly alike. Consequently, by photographing this pattern, a researcher can unequivocally identify that individual. Scientists in many locations have used this feature as the basis for long-term studies of humpback whale

A tail in the air signifies a diving whale. In summer, humpbacks generally dive for less than six minutes. In winter, however, they remain submerged for longer periods, on occasion more than half an hour.

populations, in much the same way as biologists in Africa have conducted continuous research on individually identified chimpanzees, gorillas, elephants and lions.

In both the North Atlantic and North Pacific, several thousand humpbacks have been individually identified since the 1970s, and more recently such projects have begun in other parts of the world. By patiently following individual whales over periods of years we can gain insights into their behavior, social affiliations and life histories. Sighting histories of specific females give us valuable information on reproductive rates. Whales first seen as newborn calves are observed as they grow up, reach maturity and, in the case of some young females, produce calves of their own. Some individuals are recorded by different biologists in locations separated by hundreds or even thousands of miles, giving important information on patterns of movement and migration.

In the Gulf of Maine, on the east coast of the United States, more than a thousand individuals have been documented by my institution, the Center for Coastal Studies, and other bodies. Some Gulf of Maine whales have been observed to return to the area year after year for as long as twenty years.

However, humpback whales are not easy to study. This is an animal that ranges over hundreds, even thousands of miles during the summer, makes annual migrations that take it from the poles to the tropics, lives in an environment that is frequently inhospitable and dangerous to humans, and spends most of its life out of sight underwater. Furthermore, humpbacks cannot be easily measured or weighed, are difficult to attach instrumentation to, and in most situations it is impossible visually to tell a male from a female. As if that were not bad enough, the maximum life expectancy of a humpback whale probably exceeds 50 years, far longer than the career of the average biologist!

Despite these immense difficulties, we have made great strides in our understanding in recent years. In addition, new technologies such as DNA analysis and satellite radio tagging promise to improve our knowledge even further in the near future.

A humpback rises vertically to the surface to "spyhop": the head will be raised out of the water, probably so that the animal can look around.

Nomads of the Sea

Humpback whales are truly cosmopolitan animals. They inhabit all the world's oceans, and at various times can be found from the equator almost to the poles. Like most baleen whales, humpbacks undertake extensive seasonal migrations between summer feeding grounds and the wintering areas where they mate and give birth. This annual journey takes them from the cold, productive waters of high latitudes to warm tropical seas. Once they have left the feeding grounds in late autumn, the whales cease eating and will fast for up to several months during their winter sojourn in the tropics.

The migration of the humpback whale is such a fundamental part of its life that it comes as a surprise to learn that we really do not understand its purpose. Many animals and birds migrate; most do so to exploit a locally abundant food resource, which is often linked to seasonal changes in climate. We know that this is not the case for humpback whales, since they fast while in tropical waters. Winter feeding behavior has been observed only a handful of times, and examination of innumerable animals killed by whaling showed empty stomachs and considerable weight loss during this time. Why then do humpbacks travel thousands of miles every year, only to go without food for weeks or months?

The two most popular explanations for the humpback's migration both concern energetics. The basic idea is that it costs less to travel to warm tropical seas, where heat loss is minimized, than to remain in high-latitude waters that become very cold during the winter. In one theory, all whales gain by doing this. In the other, the major benefit accrues to calves who, with their thin layer of blubber, stand a better chance of survival if they are born in the tropics.

Both theories sound intuitively reasonable, but neither is universally accepted. If calf survival is the main reason for the migration, why should other whales go to the trouble of making the trip? And are whales really better off in warm water, especially when they are not eating? Attempts to calculate the energetic gain or loss involved have produced mixed results, largely because of difficulties in estimating key factors such as metabolic rate, heat loss and food intake.

Whatever its purpose, the humpback's annual migration influences almost every aspect of the animal's life. As we will see later, the distinct geographic partitioning of the whale's year is paralleled by a marked contrast in behavior between the seasons.

There are many populations of humpback whales, and there are varying degrees of contact between them. For obvious reasons, whales from the North Atlantic never mix

with those from the North Pacific. Similarly, we would not expect humpbacks found off the coast of Australia to travel to western Africa. Furthermore, because of the seasonal opposition of the hemispheres, biologists have always assumed that humpbacks from the Antarctic never mix with those from, say, the North Pacific. This is because the southern hemisphere's summer, when humpbacks are feeding in Antarctic waters, falls at the same time as the northern hemisphere's winter, a time when North Pacific whales would have migrated to tropical waters. Six months later, when the Antarctic whales travel north to their breeding grounds, North Pacific animals have returned to high latitudes to feed. In any case, it has long been thought by many people that humpbacks rarely cross equatorial waters, so that even if the two oceanic populations were on their breeding grounds at the same time, they would never meet. All in all, the distances involved are simply too large.

Or are they? In 1990, Colombian and American biologists who had been photographing humpback whale tail patterns off the Pacific coast of South America and in the Antarctic compared their catalogues of identified individuals. To their surprise,

The humpback whale makes one of the longest migrations of any mammal. Each year humpbacks travel from high latitudes to the tropics and back, a journey that for some whales will be almost ten thousand miles long. Despite this wandering nature, they show remarkable fidelity to particular summer feeding grounds.

they found that one humpback whale photographed off the Antarctic Peninsula had later been seen off the coast of Colombia, north of the equator, a one-way distance of 8700 km, or almost 5000 nautical miles! It broke the existing record for the longest migration of any mammal, which until then had been held by the grey whale. Since then, several other individually identified humpbacks have been photographed in both places, confirming that the first "match" was not simply an errant or lost whale. Recent matches from other oceans have reinforced the idea that humpback whales everywhere are great wanderers. The mixing of whales from different hemispheres still seems unlikely given the strongly seasonal movements of the species, but we should not rule it out.

Despite their nomadic tendencies, the movements of humpback whales are not unstructured. At the end of each winter's breeding season, whales return to specific feeding grounds. In the North Atlantic, for example, some whales returning from the West Indies go to the Gulf of Maine, some to Newfoundland, while others end their migrations off Greenland, Iceland or Norway. Although there is some movement between these areas during the summer feeding season, by and large they represent discrete populations, at least until the following winter, when they will once again all mix on the breeding grounds. The area in which a particular humpback whale will feed during its life is determined by its mother, who will lead the calf back to her own feeding ground a few weeks after its birth in the tropics.

Recent DNA research has shown that such consistent return to specific feeding areas is reflected in the genetic structure of the population. Since changes in genes occur only very slowly, over the course of innumerable generations, this implies that the fidelity to particular areas must have been maintained over tens of thousands of years or longer. This is a surprising conclusion: given the humpback's known wanderlust, we might expect a gradual mixing of populations (and genes) over long periods of time, particularly since the ocean has none of the natural barriers to movement that often separate animal populations on land.

Humpbacks are insulated from the icy cold of polar waters by 15 cm (6 inches) of blubber.

Summer

In early spring, the first humpback whales begin to arrive on their feeding grounds. During the next seven to nine months, their lives will be dominated by a continual search for food. A humpback's diet can include the shrimp-like crustaceans called euphausiids (better known as krill), as well as several types of small schooling fish, including herring, sand lance, capelin and even mackerel. This varied diet is not a feature of all baleen whales. The blue whale, for example, subsists almost exclusively on krill, possibly because the whale's vast bulk brings with it biomechanical limitations that prevent it from catching faster-moving prey such as fish. The humpback's ability to exploit a broad range of species as prey is probably due in part to the greater manoeuverability afforded by its huge flippers. However, it also derives from the ingenuity of its feeding behavior.

Alone among the baleen whales, humpbacks use bubbles to trap or concentrate their prey. Perhaps the best-known method involves what is called a bubble net. The whale dives below a school of fish, and swims slowly to the surface in a spiral; as it does so, the animal releases from its blowholes columns of bubbles at regular intervals. Together, the columns form a circular or spiral barrier around the fish, preventing them from escaping and probably also packing them more tightly. When the "net" is complete, the whale lunges, with its huge mouth open, through the centre, engulfing a vast quantity of water and most of the school of fish. The water is flushed out through the baleen, and the trapped fish that remain in the mouth are swallowed.

A second technique involves the creation of a single burst of bubbles in a huge cloud. This bubble cloud may be 20 m (66 feet) in diameter; unlike the much smaller columns in a bubble net, it is probably released from the whale's mouth. The effect, however, is similar: it concentrates, traps and probably disorients prey, as well as acting as a huge screen which prevents the fish from seeing the lunging whale until it is too late.

In this aerial photo, the two main types of bubble structures that
humpbacks use to trap fish can be seen next to each other. To the left, a whale has
created the distinctive spiral shape of a bubble net. Above it to the right is the single large
burst of air that denotes a bubble cloud. Since both whales are below
the surface, neither is visible in the photo.

That humpback whales have individual characters can be clearly seen in the feeding behavior of the Gulf of Maine population. There, not only do different whales prefer nets or clouds, but they exhibit many variations on the basic themes. One of the more interesting is called "lobtail feeding". It involves the whale twisting as it dives, slapping its huge tail on the water surface on the way down, then blowing a bubble cloud and lunging through the cloud to engulf the fish. We are not sure what purpose the tail slap serves: perhaps it stuns or kills fish and thus increases the whale's "catch" during the subsequent lunge. Interestingly, this particular variation was virtually unknown in 1980, but has since spread through the population. Its appearance coincided with a shift in primary food source from herring to sand lance, and it seems that the technique evolved as an optimal means of catching the latter species. Further evidence that feeding techniques are prey-specific comes from observations of humpbacks foraging on krill, whose easier catchability is reflected in the fact that bubble structures are generally not used.

A whale can often increase its intake of food by co-operating with others in the capture of prey. However, fish or krill schools vary greatly in size, and the number of animals that can share a meal will not be constant. As a result, it is common to see the association patterns of humpback whales changing over a day, sometimes minute by minute. If we followed a feeding individual, we might find that it was alone for one feeding lunge. A few minutes later, as the whale encountered the next school of fish, it might be joined by a second animal and the two would co-operate to blow a bubble cloud or net, surfacing side by side with mouths wide open. Perhaps a third whale might join them for the next lunge, after which the three might split up and feed alone as they encountered schools too small to support more than one whale. And so on. When large amounts of food are available, many whales may feed together: during a two-day period in 1989 when millions of sand lance were concentrated in one location off Cape Cod, we witnessed the remarkable sight of up to twenty humpbacks crashing through the water surface together in what was truly a communal feast.

When prey is highly abundant, humpbacks may feed together in groups of up to twenty whales.
Some of these groups appear to be highly co-ordinated, although very few of them remain together for long periods.

With certain exceptions, this constant flux is the norm in humpback whale social behavior during the summer. Unlike many species of animals which find it advantageous or necessary to co-exist in stable groups, the ecology of humpback whales generally works against social cohesion. The huge food intake of each whale and the relatively small size of many prey schools would leave stable groups with insufficient food in many situations. A better strategy is dispersal over a feeding area and selective co-operation when large schools of prey are encountered. The tendency of most humpbacks to associate with many different individuals over the course of a summer is reinforced by their frequent need to range widely in search of prey.

In addition, the constant fear of predation which motivates many animals to form groups for communal vigilance or defence is absent in humpbacks. Although they certainly have predators, including killer whales (orcas) and perhaps sharks, attacks are rare and may be largely confined to young calves during the migration. For most of its life, a humpback need not live in fear of being someone else's next meal.

Although the exception rather than the rule, stable groups are not unknown. We have observed a few pairs of whales to remain together for periods of weeks or even months in the Gulf of Maine. More interesting is a large stable group of up to a dozen animals that has been recorded in Alaska. While membership sometimes changes, the group involves a distinct core of individuals, and has persisted for years. This is extremely unusual for this species. It seems to reflect the presence of a consistently abundant food source, and perhaps the development of co-ordinated foraging among whales with compatible feeding styles. Whether stable groups are made up primarily of relatives (a common situation in many mammals) is currently uncertain, although preliminary results from DNA analysis suggest that kinship is not an important factor in the society of humpback whales. Even mothers and calves rarely reassociate once they have separated at the end of the calf's natal year.

Despite the general flux characteristic of the associations of most whales, associations are not random. Adults tend to associate with adults, juveniles with juveniles. Males and females are found together in pairs much more commonly than we would expect by chance, although once again the great majority of these affiliations last for a few hours or less. Young whales show the pattern of social development typical of so many mammals: they are often alone when young, but

become more sociable as they grow older. By the age of sexual maturity (approximately five years for both sexes), their association patterns become largely indistinguishable from those of adults.

Although feeding is certainly the most important activity during the summer, whales do not eat continuously, and many other activities are observed at this time of year. These include the spectacular aerial behavior that has made humpbacks famous: breaching (jumping out of the water head-first), lobtailing (slamming the tail repeatedly down on the surface) and flippering (slapping their huge pectoral fins on the water). These behaviors are common and can be seen at any time of day or year, yet their function is often a mystery. It is clear that virtually all of these activities serve many different purposes. Breaching, for example, is often a sign of excitement – a sort of behavioral exclamation mark – but it may also serve to communicate position to other whales, or to shed dead skin and parasites. In many cases, a humpback may simply breach for fun: young calves breach frequently during what seems to be play. Interestingly, while breaching occurs in all weathers, it is much more likely

Humpbacks are the most acrobatic of the large whales. They breach frequently, and at all times of the year.
A whale may breach just once, or continue this spectacular behavior over and over again.

to begin when the wind is rising; we do not know why. Similarly, lobtailing and flippering are seen in many different contexts. Sometimes a whale will engage in this type of behavior when it is alone, sometimes when it is in a group.

Humpback whales also appear to play, and this behavior is not entirely confined to calves. In the Gulf of Maine, we have seen adult whales 'playing' with seaweed or floating debris. On more than one occasion, humpbacks have been seen rolling in weed, or pushing a log (in one case a telephone pole!) around with their heads. Humpbacks can also be very curious, and will often approach boats.

Do humpback whales sleep? We do not know, but it is unlikely that they do so in quite the way that we think of it. Unlike humans, all cetaceans are voluntary breathers: instead of automatically respiring, they must consciously think to breathe. This is of course an essential adaptation for a diving mammal which must exercise control over when it takes in air. Consequently, cetaceans cannot rest their entire brain at once: one half, or hemisphere, must remain alert to monitor respiratory functions. We know from studies of captive dolphins that, when they rest, only half of the brain sleeps at any time – they are literally half awake. We do not know what humpback and other baleen whales do, but it is likely to be something similar.

Although summer is the time for feeding rather than breeding, the division between the two activities is not absolute. As winter nears, hormone levels in both sexes begin to change: males produce more testosterone, and more sperm, while a female's body prepares for ovulation and possible pregnancy. In late autumn, the approach of the breeding season brings subtle shifts in behavior. Males may begin to sing, and on rare occasions are observed to compete with each other for position next to a female. These changes herald both the beginning of migration and the onset of a very different set of activities. As the whales commence their journey to the breeding grounds of the tropics, the co-operative behavior that characterized the long months of summer slowly gives way to competition as the all-important effort to secure a mate begins.

Humpbacks feed on several species of small schooling fish,
including herring, sand lance and capelin, with their baleen acting as
a huge sieve. Water is flushed out through the baleen plates, while the
coarse fringe of hair on the inside traps the fish or krill.

During a feeding lunge, the pleats on the underside of the
humpback's body expand, allowing the whale to increase the capacity of its huge mouth.
It is generally thought that a humpback whale will consume the equivalent of 3 or 4 per cent of its
own weight each day. For the largest humpback whales weighing perhaps 40 tons, this
would mean a daily food intake of between 1 and 1.5 tons.

Humpbacks are found in all the oceans of the world.
They were wandering the seas, and probably singing their haunting songs,
for several million years before the appearance of humans.

Winter

As winter sets in over the northern hemisphere, humpback whales from every ocean begin to arrive on their breeding grounds. In the West Indies, off Hawaii, off the west coast of Africa, in the island chains of southernmost Japan, and in the tropical seas of the Americas, whales from many different northern feeding grounds meet, mix and sometimes mate in the shallow waters surrounding islands or coral reefs. Six months later, southern hemisphere humpbacks will repeat this grand movement, leaving the Antarctic to winter off Madagascar, South America, Australia and the islands of the South Pacific.

The great majority of humpback calves are born at this time, and they begin their lives in an environment which is rich with the sights and sounds of other whales. Calves spend several weeks in the warm tropical water, and the mothers are among the last whales to begin the return migration to the feeding grounds at winter's end.

While mating and calving are the primary activities of the winter, other behavior is also seen. This includes the various types of aerial activity such as breaching, lobtailing and flippering, as well as curiosity and (especially among calves) play. As in summer, whales must rest at some time or other. Unlike in high latitudes, they rarely do so at the surface, probably because the tropical sun is too hot. Many whales can be seen diving for long periods, usually in the same location. We have recently determined that many of these animals are resting, sitting on or just above the bottom in shallow water, and rising to breathe every twenty or thirty minutes. It is in winter that humpbacks make their longest dives. In summer, the average dive is less than five minutes long, and dives of more than ten minutes are rather unusual. In winter, the average is ten to fifteen minutes, and many animals remain submerged for longer periods; the longest recorded dive lasted forty minutes.

The tendency of humpback whales to playfully approach boats has earned them a largely deserved reputation as gentle giants. Yet during the breeding season they are anything but gentle. During this time, male humpbacks routinely escort mature females, notably those in oestrus ("heat"). How a male determines the occurrence of oestrus in a female, and whether females actively advertize this critical state, is not known, but a female humpback in heat will generate considerable attention. Such females are at the centre of what are called competitive groups, and it is in these groups that the most spectacular interactions among males occur. Competitive groups consist of any number from three to more than twenty animals, and have generally both a clear structure and predictable dynamics. At the centre is the female, known to researchers as the nuclear animal. Next to her is a male termed the principal escort. One or more other males join this pair, and some of them will actively attempt to displace the principal escort from his position next to the female.

The first response of a principal escort who is challenged by another male is threat. Escorts often blow long streams of bubbles behind them; these probably serve as both a warning and as a screen which makes it more difficult for the challenging male to see. Males can also increase their apparent size by expanding the pleats on the underside of their bodies; although these are usually used for feeding, they can also inflate the whale's mouth to make it look more intimidating.

Should these actions fail to discourage a challenger, a male may escalate the conflict with direct aggression. Attacks can take several forms. Males use their heads, tails and entire bodies as weapons. An escort may charge directly at a challenger, slamming into him head-on or broadside. The huge tail may be slashed violently and repeatedly through the water to strike another male.

Such conflicts may be brief, with a challenger easily discouraged or an escort quickly displaced. Or they may be protracted: we have followed active competitive groups for many hours, with bursts of aggressive activity interspersed with quieter periods when the participants rest, recover and prepare for the next bout. The groups are dynamic, and often gain and lose members: some whales give up and leave while others are attracted to the action and come from many kilometers away to join the fray. Not all participants are active. Many whales simply follow along on the group's periphery; these are probably smaller or younger whales who dare not challenge the escort for his position, but stay in the slim hope that they can exploit an opening when the main participants are exhausted. Fights in competitive groups, while spectacular, are never fatal. While visible wounds are common, serious injuries are probably rare.

Humpbacks breach for many different reasons. Possible functions include communicating
position to other whales, ridding themselves of dead skin or parasites, and expressing excitement.
Whales of all ages breach, although the behavior is particularly common amongst calves.
In some instances, a breaching humpback can completely clear the water.

A mother and her newborn calf glide through the sunlit water of the tropics.
Underwater visibility is much better here than on the feeding grounds,
where productivity generally makes the water murky.

Recent work we have conducted in the West Indies suggests an interesting twist to the competitive group story. We have occasionally observed pairs of animals entering or leaving competitive groups together, and appearing to work together against the principal escort. When we determined the sex of these animals using DNA analysis of skin biopsies, they proved to be pairs of males. Thus it seems likely that males sometimes form coalitions to displace an escort.

A final male strategy involves escorting a mother with a newborn calf and waiting for her to come into oestrus. Escorting may be a strategy adopted largely by males who are not strong enough to challenge others in competitive groups (although these groups often form around such mother-calf-escort trios). Given a choice between a mother and a non-reproducing female, we would expect a male to choose the latter, for two reasons. First, because not many females produce two calves in two years, only a minority of escorted mothers will represent good prospects for mates. Second, lactation is so expensive of effort that a mother will be in relatively poor condition by the time she has weaned her calf the following winter; if she is simultaneously pregnant, this second calf may be weaker and have a lower probability of survival. Consequently, courting a mother is probably not a very good option, and one which may be pursued largely by "inferior" males.

What of females? Do they swim along passively in the midst of all the violence, and submissively mate with the eventual winner when a competitive group finally breaks up? Female behavior is very difficult to study in a species which conducts much of its activity underwater; indeed, neither copulation nor birth has ever been observed. However, it is unlikely that females meekly accept the outcome of male-male contests. As is the case for all mammals, there is a huge difference in the reproductive costs borne by male and female humpback whales. Males must sometimes fight for females, but once they have mated they are essentially free to seek other mates. By contrast, once a female humpback whale has conceived, she must undergo almost a year of pregnancy followed by ten months of nursing, and all without any assistance from a male. In light of this, it is probable that females are much more choosy than males about their mates.

We have little hard evidence to investigate the question of how female humpbacks

A male humpback in singing posture. Whales will sometimes sing for hours, or even days.

select mates, but certain observations suggest some possibilities. If females choose a male based upon heritable qualities that may benefit her offspring, then the competitive group provides an obvious forum for assessment of potential partners, since size, strength and manoeuverability are key factors in these contests.

Females certainly do not always passively accept the advances of males. In our studies in the West Indies, we have sometimes discovered that the aggressive whale at the centre of a competitive group is not male, but female. In one case a female repeatedly struck a whale that we recognized as a six-year-old male from the Gulf of Maine. At six, this animal would have only recently become sexually mature. Thus it seems likely that the female had as little interest in him as a woman would have in the advances of a teenage boy, and made this quite clear with an aggressive response. In other cases, we have observed females lobtailing or flippering next to a male, and this activity has sometimes resulted in the formation of a competitive group, with other males coming from some distance away. It is possible that this behavior serves to solicit challenges to an unwanted escort from other males.

A final possibility which has been suggested as a means for females to judge the quality of males leads us to one of the most interesting and famous aspects of the humpback whale: its song.

In biology, a song is any two or more notes that are repeated in a pattern. The simple two-note chirp of a cricket is technically a song, because it follows a pattern. Bird song is much more varied and is familiar to us all. Humpback whales also sing, and their songs are probably the most complex in the animal kingdom.

A humpback whale song consists of units of sound which combine to form what is known as a phrase. The repetition of a phrase is called a theme, and a song will be made up of a number of separate themes (songs recorded by biologists have contained anything from two to nine). Themes are sung in a specific order, and the entire song will last anywhere from a few minutes to half an hour. Once completed, the whale will return to the beginning and start again. Whales will sing for hours, and in some cases may sing continuously for days at a time.

All the humpback whales from a single population sing the same song, but different oceans have different songs. If you record two or more songs anywhere in the North Atlantic during the winter, the structure and content will be the same, but very different from songs sung at the same time in the North Pacific. What is remarkable about this is that the song changes progressively with time. Over a period of several years, songs from the same ocean become recognizably different, yet somehow all of the whales manage to keep up with the changes. How this is accomplished is not known, although in deep water the lower-frequency portions of the song can be heard over distances of hundreds of miles.

What is the function of this remarkable vocal display? That only male humpbacks sing, and that singing occurs primarily during the winter, argues persuasively that it is related to breeding. Males of many species, from insects to frogs to birds, sing, and this activity is generally used as a means of attracting females. In many cases it also serves to announce territory, to maintain spacing between adjacent males, or to advertize the fitness of the singer. It is very likely that humpback whale song is no different. In an aquatic environment, visual displays are useless except at close range. However, since sound travels both better and faster in water than in air, the sea is an ideal medium for acoustic "advertizing".

Singing males are almost always alone, but will sometimes be joined by another whale. In some cases, the joining animal is male, and a brief altercation may occur. At other times, the approaching whale is female, and it is quite possible that these interactions represent instances of females investigating or perhaps even choosing a potential mate. But at present we cannot be sure, largely because the significant elements of such encounters take place below the surface, out of our sight.

The song of the humpback whale is undeniably a hauntingly beautiful phenomenon, as anyone who has had the fortune to hear it surrounding them in the water can attest. Yet it contains many mysteries. Why does it change? Why is it so complex? Is the change in the song led by successful males, who must constantly introduce novelty into its structure in order to stand out from the imitations of others? We do not know.

*A singer in clear waters off Hawaii. Water is an excellent medium for the transmission of sound,
and in deep water the low-frequency portions of a humpback's song may be audible over literally hundreds of miles.*

One Whale's Life

The year is 1984, and it is late autumn in the Gulf of Maine. The water is already cold, and there is a snap in the air that foretells of the approaching winter. A few miles off the coast of Cape Cod, a large female humpback whale is feeding on schools of small fish. She is known to local researchers as Salt, after the prominent white scarring, like a sprinkling of salt, on her dorsal fin. They have photographed her familiar black and white tail pattern hundreds of times since she was first observed in 1975.

Salt's age is unknown, but she is probably no more than ten or eleven years old at this time. Every spring she has returned here, and twice before, in 1980 and 1983, she has appeared with a new calf at her side. Now, she is pregnant once more, and soon she will begin the long journey to the tropics. It is there that the calf that she is carrying was conceived the previous winter, and there that it will be born. In these last few days before she leaves the cold waters of the north, she will eat as much as she can. The reserves of fat that she has built up all summer will be used partly to sustain herself during the long fast that she must make in the coming months. But much of this vast store will go to producing milk for her calf after it is born. Inside Salt's womb, the foetus is growing rapidly; it will double in size during the final two months of gestation. The foetal growth rates of baleen whales are the fastest of any mammal, some twenty times that of primates like humans.

One day in November, responding perhaps to the fading light or to some cue within her body, she turns south and begins a migration that will take her across 2300 km (1300 miles) of open ocean to the reefs and islands of the West Indies. She does not linger on the way: guided by a navigational system that we do not understand, she will travel for about three weeks to a final destination somewhere in the Antilles. Perhaps it will be Silver Bank, the largest of all humpback whale breeding grounds. This limestone platform 80 km (50 miles) north of the Dominican Republic rises out of 2000 m of water to within 30 m of the surface, and it is fringed on one edge by a barrier reef. The dense coral provides

Humpback calves stay very close to their mothers, especially when they are very young.

protection from rolling easterly swells generated by the constant trade winds, and it is believed that many female humpbacks give birth in the sheltered water behind the reef.

The birth, which occurs in February, is probably quick. The calf, a female, is immediately able to swim by herself. Pushed by Salt, she rises to the surface to take her first breath. Shortly after, she begins to nurse. Her mother's two mammary glands, which lie on the underside of her body towards the tail, each contain a compressor muscle. Consequently, unlike land mammals, the mother actively pumps milk into the mouth of the hungry calf. The milk is more than one-third fat (in comparison, the fat content of human milk is 2%). Four meters (14 feet) long and weighing three-quarters of a ton at birth, the calf will grow rapidly in the year in which she remains in her mother's care. But, the cost to Salt of producing up to fifty gallons a day of such rich milk is high. By the time that she has weaned her daughter ten months from now, she will have lost ten tons, or almost one third of her entire body weight.

The environment in which the calf spends the first weeks of her life is full of light and sound. The water is warm, sunlit and clear. All around the calf hears the singing of male humpback whales. At the peak of the winter breeding season, Silver Bank is host to perhaps three thousand humpbacks from all over the North Atlantic, and more than half are male. The chorus of their singing echoes through the surrounding water, day and night. Sometimes a lone male will join Salt and her calf, hoping that she will come into heat again. This year, she will not. Nonetheless, many males escort her, and sometimes they compete aggressively for the privilege. The calf swims close to her mother during these fights, as the escorting male slams broadside into a challenger, or slashes him with his great tail.

By mid-March the calf has grown substantially, and Salt and her daughter begin the long migration north. On this journey, the calf will learn the routes that she will take to and from the feeding grounds in future years, when she has left her mother and must make the trip on her own. As they head north, passing over the great ocean depths, the water slowly begins to feel colder.

The pair arrive off Cape Cod in the second week of April. A few days later, they are

Mural

Salt

Talon

Liner

*In the Gulf of Maine, researchers give each humpback whale a name.
This is always based upon some prominent marking, such as their tail fluke pattern,
making identification in the field easier.*

We know that humpback whales travel hundreds of miles between locally productive areas because known individuals are routinely observed in widely separated locations, sometimes over intervals of just a few days.

spotted by researchers, who are delighted to see that Salt has both successfully survived another winter, and given birth to a third calf. They name the calf Thalassa, after the Greek word for "sea". One day the calf rolls over playfully next to their boat, and the researchers see from the lobe in its genital area that it is female. Both of Salt's previous calves were males.

All summer, Salt and Thalassa roam the Gulf of Maine. Generally, they travel alone, but sometimes they join other whales for short periods of time. One day they see Crystal, Salt's first son; but mother and former calf do not reassociate, and go their separate ways. Often they are among large concentrations of humpbacks, and the calf also becomes familiar with other cetaceans. Huge, sleek fin whales cruise by, sometimes with dolphins riding on the bow wave created by their massive heads. Groups of  pilot whales are encountered offshore, diving together to search for squid. Once, swimming across a deep-water channel at the edge of the continental shelf, they meet a large male sperm whale which breathes many times at the surface before once more diving far down into the lightless depths below.

Salt feeds frequently on sand lance or herring, and sometimes on krill. For a long time, Thalassa takes only milk, and must often amuse herself while her mother eats. But late in the summer she begins to imitate the bubble clouds that Salt blows to trap fish. Soon after she takes her first meal of fish, and for several weeks she will eat both milk and solid food.

By November, Thalassa has grown to a length of 8 m (26 feet). Soon, Salt will begin another migration to the West Indies, and at some point during the coming winter, mother and daughter will separate. Salt will conceive again, and will give birth to another son the following year.

Like her mother, Thalassa will live through the continuing cycle of the seasons, feeding in the cold waters of the north and travelling to the tropics in winter. The researchers who named her will see her return each year to the Gulf of Maine and

watch as she grows up. By the time that she is five years old, she will be sexually mature, although she will continue to grow and will not reach physical maturity until perhaps ten years later.

It is early morning on a spring day in 1992. In the waters north of Cape Cod, scientists see the tall blows of a humpback whale rising into the cold air a mile ahead of their small research vessel. As they get closer to the whale, they are excited to see that the animal is accompanied by a calf, whose spout is too small and indistinct to be seen from a distance. As always, they are eager to learn the identity of the mother who has produced this latest addition to the Gulf of Maine population. They position the boat behind the animals and wait for the sounding dive, hoping that the mother will raise her tail and show them the pattern that holds the key to her identity. With great anticipation they watch as she takes five breaths, then a sixth. They see her huge flippers pushed out to brace herself for the dive, then her back rolls and her wide tail rises gracefully into the air before them. As the pattern of black and white underneath becomes visible, a chorus of cheers erupts from the boat. The whale is Thalassa, and she has returned with her first calf.

Conservation

Without a doubt, the single largest cause of mortality among whales in recent times has been whaling. The intensive exploitation of the great whales this century probably wiped out more than 95% of the humpbacks that once roamed freely through the world's oceans. The numbers for other species are similarly depressing. If our civilization ever evolves to a more enlightened level, it must surely look back upon this wanton destruction of some of the earth's most magnificent creatures as one of the greatest of our many environmental crimes.

Whaling has a long history. Coastal people often made use of stranded whales as a great store of meat, oil and other products. At least four thousand years ago, whales were actively hunted off the coast of Persia. Slow coastal species such as the right whale and the humpback were the targets of early whalers; the faster rorquals were generally beyond the reach of their technology.

The first record of a humpback whale being killed dates from 1608 off the American island of Nantucket, although there is no doubt that the species had been hunted in many places long before that. American whalers were particularly involved in "humpbacking". In the last century, vessels from Cape Cod regularly took humpbacks in the waters of the southeastern Caribbean and off the west coast of Africa. Some ships ventured as far as the Pacific or the Indian Ocean, although many of these were primarily interested in sperm whales, whose oil was more valuable than that of the humpback.

While historic whaling operations undoubtedly did great damage to some populations of whales, slow vessels and hand-held harpoons could accomplish only so much. The introduction in the late 19th century of the explosive harpoon and the steam engine brought all whales under the gun for the first time. In 1904, the world's richest whaling ground, the Antarctic, was opened up. Factory ships permitted

Approximately a quarter of a million humpback whales have been killed by the whaling industry. Today, the humpback seems to be making a major recovery in most parts of its range.

whaling fleets to stay at sea for long periods, and to rapidly process large numbers of whales. The slaughter was unparalleled: two million whales of many species were killed in the Southern Ocean alone. By the time that humpback whales were given worldwide protection from hunting in 1966, almost a quarter of a million had been killed and the great southern hemisphere populations had been reduced to a fraction of their original size. The same was true for other species. Recently, it was revealed that the Soviet Union secretly killed over 100,000 more whales than they reported. Humpbacks suffered more than any other from this illegal slaughter: reporting 2,710, the Soviets had actually killed more than 48,000.

The tubercles were known as "stovebolts" to whalers, who fancifully imagined that they held the whale's head together.

Today, however, whaling is not a serious concern for humpback whales. Commercial whaling (legal or otherwise) for this species has effectively ceased. Although a few native operations still kill humpbacks, and there is evidence that "pirate" whaling operations exist, it is unlikely that they take enough whales to threaten any population.

We do not know how many humpback whales existed worldwide prior to the onset of sustained whaling, but the number was certainly in the hundreds of thousands. Estimating the abundance of a wide-ranging, difficult-to-study species is not an easy matter, and most population estimates must be regarded as educated guesses. However, all the signs point to the idea that humpbacks are making a strong comeback in most places. Indeed, this species seems remarkably resilient. In most places, our studies consistently record many new whales, and many new calves, each

Left alone, the humpback appears to be capable of recovering from even the huge excesses of commercial whaling. Its relatively high reproductive rate, early attainment of sexual maturity, and its flexibility concerning what it eats, are probably the major reasons for this resilience.

Probably the greatest threat to humpback whales today comes from entanglements in fishing gear.
Each year many humpbacks, and countless other sea creatures, die from such entrapments.

year. Even the Antarctic population, once heavily damaged by whaling, is beginning to rebound: scientists working along the coasts of Australia report a consistent increase in the numbers of migrating whales each season.

While optimism for the future of the humpback whale does not seem unwarranted, such hopefulness should be tempered with a measure of caution. Whaling may have ceased, but the world's oceans are far from being free of perils.

Entanglement in fishing gear is a huge problem for a host of marine species, including humpbacks. In a few places, such as Newfoundland, the Gulf of Maine and the coast of Oman, scientists and others have mounted an effort to rescue large whales from such entanglements. We would like to be able to extend this effort to smaller marine mammals, but, regrettably, most dolphins, porpoises and seals drown when they are caught. Large whales, because of their sheer size, can

The humpback's tendency to approach boats was often their downfall during whaling days.

sometimes swim away with the entire net wrapped around them. In many cases, the net subsequently makes it difficult for the whale to move and feed, and some animals suffer a prolonged death from starvation.

The other major issue of concern is pollution. We have used the sea as a dump for noxious chemicals, sewage and other waste for hundreds of years. The great system of currents that ultimately connects all oceans has circulated contaminants such as DDT and PCBs from the poles to the tropics. Unfortunately, the mechanisms by which such pollutants act upon organisms and ecosystems are highly complex.

This makes it exceedingly difficult to demonstrate cause and effect relationships; in the absence of such proofs, managers and politicians are reluctant to act.

Recently, mass mortalities in some marine mammal populations have raised concerns about environmental toxins. Die-offs of North Sea seals, and of dolphins in the Mediterranean, were clearly caused by a viral epidemic. However, many scientists, noting the often extraordinarily high concentrations of PCBs and other contaminants in the tissues of the animals concerned, have suggested that these may have suppressed immune response and thus allowed the virus to sweep unresisted through the population. Because of the complexity of the topic, this remains unproven. However, it seems an increasingly plausible explanation, and raises a large red flag which we would do well to heed.

A whale displays the raked tooth marks on its tail that probably come from an attack by killer whales.

Baleen whales are theoretically at lower risk from such toxins because they eat further down on the food chain than most odontocetes and seals; consequently, contaminants should be less concentrated in their food and their tissues. Recent research has confirmed this prediction. However, mammals are particularly vulnerable to toxins because these chemicals are frequently transferred through milk from a mother to her nursing offspring. Although this lowers the contaminant burden in the mother's body, it means that each generation will begin with an increased level of pollutants. We do not know whether such transgenerational accummulation will eventually result in major problems for

Humpbacks are among the most curious of the large whales, a trait that has made them popular with whalewatchers.

humpback whales and other mysticetes, and more research on this subject is urgently needed.

A mass mortality of humpbacks off Cape Cod in 1987 involved at least 15 animals, and other deaths probably went unrecorded when dead whales drifted out to sea. The cause was poisoning by saxitoxin, which is associated with "red tide" events. The toxin was concentrated in the livers of mackerel eaten by the whales. Although red tides are a naturally occurring event, their frequency appears to be related to freshwater and sewage run-off from coastal development. While this is the only known case of a red tide affecting baleen whales, the rapid pace of development in the coastal zone may bring more problems of this type in future years.

The future of the humpback whale is inextricably linked with that of its habitat: put simply, if we cannot save the seas, we will not save the whales. Humans have long looked out at the vast ocean and thought of it as an entity of limitless size and power, upon which the works of mankind could have but little impact. Too often, and too conveniently, it has also been regarded as a barren waste, devoid of the diversity which surrounds us on the familiar land. We know now that neither belief is correct. Our fisheries devastate populations and alter ecosystems. The noise of our innumerable ships is heard everywhere. Our pollutants are found in the tissues of marine organisms both great and small, in even the most remote corners of the sea. And far from being a desert, the ocean is teeming with life that rivals the most productive tropical rain forest in its diversity and richness. If cetaceans are to have a future, we must cease to view the seas as a limitless dumping ground, or as an unending store of resources to be plundered at will.

It now seems that we stopped whaling just in time for humpback whales, and we may yet live to see them attain some semblance of their former abundance. It would truly be a tragedy if we drew back from the edge of the precipice, only to destroy the habitat upon which the continued existence of this, and so many other species, ultimately depends.

Humpback Whale Facts

Scientific name:	*Megaptera novaeangliae*
Average length (adult female):	13 m (43 feet)
(adult male):	12.5 m (41 feet)
(newborn calf):	4.2 m (14 feet)
Average adult weight (female):	25-30 tons
Breadth of tail:	4.6 m (15 feet)
Length of flipper:	4 m (13 feet)
Longevity:	40-50 years

Reproduction – Both males and females are sexually mature at five years, although males may not actively breed until later. The gestation period is approximately 11.5 months. Females give birth to a single calf every two or three years, although consecutive-year calving is possible. Calves leave their mothers after one year.

Distribution – Humpback whales are found in all the world's oceans. They feed in high latitudes during the spring, summer and autumn, and migrate to tropical mating and calving grounds for the winter.

Recommended Reading

Wings In The Sea, The Humpback Whale by Lois K. Winn and Howard E. Winn, University Press of New England, London, 1985. A highly readable popular account of the biology and life of humpback whales.

Whales and Dolphins by Anthony Martin and a team of experts, Salamander Books Ltd. London, 1990. A thoroughly researched and beautifully illustrated overview of cetaceans.

The Natural History of Whales and Dolphins by Peter Evans, Christopher Helm (Publishers) Ltd, London, 1987. An in-depth review of the biology of cetaceans.

Biographical Note

Phil Clapham is a Research Associate at the Smithsonian Institution (National Museum of Natural History) in Washington DC, where he lives and works. He is also a Senior Scientist with the Center for Coastal Studies in Massachusetts, where he has directed a long-term study of humpback whales. Cornish by birth, he holds a Ph.D. in biology from the University of Aberdeen.